SAFEHOLD

THE DREAMSEEKER
POETRY SERIES

Books in the DreamSeeker Poetry Series, intended to make available fine writing by Anabaptist-related poets, are published by Cascadia Publishing House under the DreamSeeker Books imprint and often copublished with Herald Press. Cascadia oversees content of these poetry collections in collaboration with the DreamSeeker Poetry Series Editor Jeff Gundy (Jean Janzen volumes 1-4) as well as in consultation with its Editorial Council and the authors themselves.

Also worth noting are two poetry collections that would likely have been included in the series had it been in existence then:

DreamSeeker Books also continues to release occasional high-caliber collections of poems outside of the DreamSeeker Poetry Series:

SAFEHOLD

POEMS BY
Ann Hostetler

DreamSeeker Poetry Series, Volume 15

DreamSeeker Books
TELFORD, PENNSYLVANIA

an imprint of
Cascadia Publishing House LLC

Cascadia Publishing House orders, information, reprint permissions:
contact@CascadiaPublishingHouse.com
1-215-723-9125
126 Klingerman Road, Telford PA 18969
www.CascadiaPublishingHouse.com

Safehold
Copyright © 2018 by Cascadia Publishing House LLC
All rights reserved
DreamSeeker Books is an imprint of Cascadia Publishing House LLC
Library of Congress Catalog Number: 2018043267
ISBN 13: 978-1-68027-010-5; ISBN 10: 1-68027-010-9
Book design by Cascadia Publishing House
Cover design by Gwen M. Stamm

Versions of poems in this collection have appeared in various outlets. For a complete listing, see Acknowledgments section, back of book.

Library of Congress Cataloguing-in-Publication Data
Names: Hostetler, Ann Elizabeth, author.
Title: Safehold / poems by Ann Hostetler.
Description: Telford, Pennsylvania : DreamSeeker Books, [2018] | Series:
  Dreamseeker poetry series ; volume 15
Identifiers: LCCN 2018043267| ISBN 9781680270105 (trade pbk. : alk.
paper) |
  ISBN 1680270109 (trade pbk. : alk. paper)
Classification: LCC PS3608.O835 A6 2018 | DDC 811/.6--dc23
LC record available at https://lccn.loc.gov/2018043267

23 22 21 20 19 18   10 9 8 7 6 5 4 3 2 1

For my family

CONTENTS

Part One: Songs for Ancestors

Part Two: Travelers

Part Three:
Sonnets for the Amish Girls of Nickel Mines

Part Four: Unexpected Guest

Part Five: Legacy

two by two in the ark
of the ache of it.

—Denise Levertov

Part One

SONGS FOR ANCESTORS

HEIRLOOMS

I wonder as I dig what fruit will grow
from seedlings named
Green Zebra and Golden Jubilee,
wonder why I scrape dirt
around their roots when I can buy
tomatoes at the farmer's market.

Hands deep in soil, I squat. Scent rises
from the earth between my thighs. Sweat
streams down my husband's torso as he spades,
shovel chunking through grit. Our toddler
stoops, a tip of hair gathered at his nape.
Retrieving pebbles, he finds what is his.

All my life I've tried to live as though
the body were the soul. As though planting
and reaping were prayer. Our bodies a perishable
husk to feed the soul's kernel, the earth
absorbing what's left, seeding
next year's volunteers.

PORTRAIT OF THE ARTIST

I stare into the glass across
the dresser: all doubles:

the coins in the
bowl, Grecian,
the warm lamps on
either side;
her golden hand mirror,
his brush and cologne.

Above the bowl's rim,
one girl, two dark eyes,
counts her breath.
She doesn't seem to be me.

A woman behind her
stands braiding,
hands dancing, her wedding
ring: tossing the light.

BEING SEEN

My mother's eyes would trace my shape;
when she thought I wasn't looking,
I could feel her gaze on me—appraising,

adjusting, soothing like a tongue worries
a cold sore in the mouth. She was an artist:
my mother's eyes would trace my shape.

No harm in looking—eyes do not touch—
yet her looking made me feel my edges.
I could feel her gaze on me—appraising,

an object she owned, she'd made. But
when I sat for my portrait, amidst objects
I chose, my mother's eyes would trace

an antique primer clasped to my chest,
ballet shoes, a vase with a purple sprig—
I could feel her gaze—appraising—

as she focused on her painting.
When she was painting, I felt free
of the eyes that traced my shape,
of the feeling of her gaze on me.

SELF-PORTRAIT
October 2014, after Arnaut Daniel

I am Ann Hostetler, born in Mt. Pleasant, Pennsylvania,
to two smart people who loved God and books,
eldest of three, mother of four, grandmother
of two, wife of one. This Week of the Dead
in Oaxaca I celebrate my father's birthday—
he would be 96—and mourn the passing
of Galway Kinnell and Uncle Marc. Today I am
alive in Oaxaca, a payer of bills. A fortunate traveler.
A student of Spanish and yoga. And today: I will
stand on my head for one minute, learn to be at peace
with animals, meet in person all of those whose words
I treasure, play with paints and canvas, write
ten brilliant books of poetry. But just now,
I will keep taking pictures with my mind's eye.

MARKET

Don't you just love tomatoes?
The words burst from my mouth

and a man in my father's raincoat
turns to reveal a face I've never seen.

I am five and afraid,
so I run to the next stall

where my father is putting
potatoes in a sack.

I say nothing
about the tomatoes, about

how their red magic can make you
talk to strangers.

AUGUST CONSOLATION

The Queen Anne's lace in the vase
is limp. My drawing isn't working. I close
my sketchbook. I'll never be an artist.
In the living room my sister practices
her violin with strong, even strokes,
not quite shrieking. Everything is boring
since I came back from Boston.
I met a cool girl there, her bangs so long
they covered her eyes. I loved the way
she tossed her hair. In the kitchen sink
my sister's cereal bowl sits half full
of water, spoon inside. Mother doesn't
allow dishes in the sink. I leave it there.
Through the window's sliding screen
a puff of breeze. I look up the hill to
the neighbor's ugly silver cyclone fence.
I want to go back to Boston. My sister
sounds her strong, even strokes, not quite
shrieking. A ripe tomato from our garden
on the counter catches my eye. I slice it
and put it on a plate. A sprinkle of salt brings
its juices to the surface. I set it beside
the sketchbook and drooping flower.
Maybe I'll run a restaurant.

CHOOSING SIDES

"Methodist," I used to say
when the neighborhood kids asked,

because the word began with "M."
Once I nodded yes to "Mormon"

and gained a friend. She invited me
to dinner. When her parents asked, I confessed.

"Mennonites are a lot like Mormons," they said
and offered me homemade meatballs after grace.

At recess, when the kids played war, I chose
the German side, because my father grew up speaking

Pennsylvania Dutch. "Not that kind of German,"
he said. After explaining Hitler, the Nazis, the extermination

of the Jews, the two world wars, he told me
the story of Edith Cavell, World War I nurse

who faced a firing squad for helping
wounded soldiers from both sides.

What's wrong with helping both
sides, I asked. Didn't Jesus heal

the sick and teach us to love our enemies?
Would my enemies put down their guns

If I told them I was Mennonite?

MARTYR'S MIRRORS

"We are more than the sum total of our wounds."
The priest's voice echoes through the nearly empty
nave of St. Paul's Episcopal.

From the Tiffany windows, installed in better times,
angels with lilac wings and golden hair
gesture toward a city of light.

I remember Anabaptist ancestors
who desecrated images in cathedrals,
who entered the flames singing.

Wrong to imagine them pictured here
with bonfire, rack, tongue screw emblazoned
in sun-licked colors. Images pressed

into my brain as they were pressed
onto rag paper centuries ago,
in the book father brought home.

to show us how others suffered
to keep the faith. Last night
my daughter calls from 12,000 miles away

to tell me she slit her arm
from elbow to wrist, but now she's okay.
The priest's words flood back.

Who taught her that pain validates?
Wounds are not writing.
The body is not a book..

People are murdered—not martyred—
unless language makes it so.

SETTLING THE SCORE

After my father showed me the engravings
of executions in the *Martyr's Mirror*, and I learned
the awful truth about who'd killed my ancestors,

I ran down the hill and into our Catholic
neighbor's yard. All out of breath I broke the news
to my friend: your ancestors killed my ancestors!

She glanced at me with her green eyes, then
looked away. After a moment of silence, she invited
me onto her red swing set, and we played all afternoon.

CATECHISM

From the dusty bicycle trailer behind me,
she calls out: "Momma, what are eyes?"
    "They are for seeing."
    "Can you have eyes and not see?"
    "Then you are called blind."

Scarlet tanagers dart
among stands of birch and pine.
Bridal veil tumbles wild
in the overgrowth between lots
where mansions have begun
to appear. A young doe
turns her head to watch us pass.

"What is it called when you have ears but can't hear?"
    "Deaf."
    "Death?"
    "Deaf-f-f-f."
    "Death?"

I prop the bike against the kickstand
and send her off with a kiss at the door.
Back home, I find a fledgling caught
in the trailer's wheel, lift its taut,
dried body from the spoke.

MY DAUGHTER LOVES HER CHILDREN'S LONG HAIR

Every cell produced by their bodies precious to her,
their eyes hidden like berries shining in a thicket.

I want to uncover them from the tangles
so they do not have to tilt their heads

to look out at the world. "Old people want
to see your eyes," I tell them, joking. But

when my grandmother lifted my chin upward
with the surprising force of her bony hand

to examine my eyes, noticing one was larger, my
face grew hot, and I began to doubt myself.

"If you pull your hair away from your forehead
people can see your beautiful eyes," my mother

would tell me when I hid behind my preteen bangs.
I didn't want to be seen—I hardly knew who I was.

But my grandchildren?
I want to watch their clear lenses taking in

the light, reflections on the grass, their toys. They
toss their heads away from the brush of my fingers,

hair falling back into their eyes.

TOO BIG FOR WORDS

He wanders the house no longer able to read
the books he's spent a lifetime writing. Every day

I write and run on the millrace path behind his house,
then stop to sit with him on the back porch

and watch the other runners—stooped or vigorous—
as they pass beyond our line of sight.

If only I could write this down, he lifts his wasted arms,
it would be incredible. You're like a medicine man

with your dreams and visions, I reply. Back home, I tear apart
the bedroom, set up a writing space by the windows,

a fortress of books, paper, and a blank computer screen.
It's a big iceberg and its breaking up, he tells me.

I fell down the stairs looking for the policemen.
There's just so much conflict in the world.

This morning he couldn't lift his foot to put his trousers on,
couldn't find the chair behind him when he wanted to sit.

Shall we walk to the porch? I take his arm.
Did you say the Nebraska book is over the hill? Then,

He's really got the pig by the tail, but then we're all in the pigpen.
Mother joins us on the porch. *What's your name?* he asks.

We decide it's time, lead him to the car.
He crawls into the back seat because he can't remember how

to sit in the front. In his new, bare room he turns
and says, *Maybe we should go out to a mountain someplace.*

Two weeks after his funeral the towers fall in New York.
He must have felt something coming, a thing too big for words.

TRANSFIGURATION

I entered his room for the last time,
to see only a shell—broken—his head
thrown back, mouth open—as though
something hatched and took flight.

Just that morning I had rubbed
his ankles with oil, but now
his legs were stiff to the touch.
Purple pooled under tissue paper skin

as inner walls gave way, the process
of return beginning. At the hospital entrance,
I met the women weeping—mother, sister, niece,
pastor—who told me the story of his last

breath, which I imagine now:
my sister plays her violin—*Cast thy Burden
Upon the Lord*—and after days
of uphill breathing his face reflects

a moment of sheer delight—*Christ
We Do All Adore Thee*. I carry
this story with me like a cloak.
that gets bigger and warmer
each time I wear it.

THE SACRAMENT OF SHOES

When she came home from the hospital,
ankles and feet so swollen she couldn't
wear the soft, slender shoes she loved,
I sat on the footstool, one palm on her sole,
one palm on her instep, and smoothed her feet with oil.
Her ankles looked like snakes that had swallowed rabbits.
My fingertips pressed pale ovals into the swelling
to coax the fluids through. I read about
reflexology, so I could locate the nerve endings
in her sole, and pray with my fingers
that her weary heart would grow strong.
I thought of Jesus washing his disciples' feet,
but I didn't feel saintly, only grateful.
She was the host,
and sitting at her feet a taste of paradise.
Every time I left her I repeated,
"The host dissolving on my tongue."
When we cleaned out her closet,
none of us could fit into
her beautiful shoes.

FLIGHT PATTERNS

At the edge of the marsh the redwing blackbirds
swoop onto the tips of cattails, call to each other

as they pair for nesting. I wheel her chair
into a patch of sun so she can watch them with me,

just as I used to wheel her chair down the hall
to the wedge of light pouring from the propped-

open fire door when she grew too weary to walk.
Today the wheels glide through the tussocks

of bluestem and boggy dips so she's not shaken,
only slightly chilled from the raw air. I snatch

the mohair stole from the couch, the peach one
she used to wrap herself in on winter evenings.

The birds dart and dive, full and free, their landings
precise. Red winks from their wings

as the brittle stalks sway. From her apartment
window she used to watch the swans in the artificial

pond, their wings clipped so they would stay.
Here, today, she stands to stretch her wings,

dissolve into the motes of light filtering
through the lace of newly leafing trees.

OCTOBER LEAVES

Once it seemed so important—
who would inherit great-grandma's cherry table,
the pump organ with red cloth
showing through carved orifices,
the grand piano, father's desk, mother's pearls,
the set of illustrated classics
lodged in the walnut bookcase
he gave her for an engagement present
because a diamond was too worldly.

Filled with fairy tales about legacies,
my sisters and I would argue as children,
like three old crones, over the spoilage
of our parents' hoard. Already practicing,
we'd portion out the goods we all wanted.
Now their wood and paper inheritance
sits heavy in our living rooms.

The rest we carry with us,
like Blake's illustrations of Pilgrim
that show his burden bulging
in the muscles of his back,
the only inheritance that matters, love
shared between and among us,
alive in our breath.

SACRED HARP SINGING IN MID-JULY

We hear the humming as soon as we close
the car doors. At the entrance of the New
Testament Baptist Church there's a crowd.
Honeybees at the mouth of the hive. We
shoulder our way into a resonator
box of sound. There's just enough room to settle
in the back row with my daughter, her partner,
and their new baby. An older man and a boy stand
in the center and keep the beat with bent right arms
while singers on all four sides pump the bellows
of the breath. Around us people in head coverings,
suspenders, plain suits, tank tops, T-shirts, shorts, makeup,
nose rings, sing full-throated in four-part harmony
about death and salvation. My daughter does not know
the words, and I cannot open my mouth for fear
that the pain of my grandparents' shunning will leap out
in a wail or shriek. My new granddaughter sleeps
in her plastic car seat, propped on the back
of the pew so she can get some air.

BIRTHDAY DINNERS

I.

I pour a single glass of chilled white wine
and set it on the table in your honor.
You would be eighty-two today if your heart
had been stronger. From the garden I pluck
handfuls of ripe raspberries. I remember you
telling how your birthday was forgotten in the
press of the berry harvest. Yet how you loved
to eat fresh raspberry pie with whipped cream.
Tonight, I am remembering you with
a whole wild salmon brushed with Asian Sesame
sauce, even though only my youngest child
is at home and the house a mess. But I have cleared
the table, mother. I have tossed fresh greens.
You will not have to eat alone tonight.

II.

No more have I set a solitary
place for you then the phone rings. It's my daughter
who wants to know how to cut the breasts off
of a chicken. Put that chicken in the fridge,
I tell her, and come over for salmon.
Now we've made the table larger, spread
a cloth and placed your great-granddaughter
across from you. To keep her out of trouble
I've taught her to shell peas and she's taken
to the task with zeal, her fine brown hair

so much like yours, escaping all barrettes
and bands. She names the peas, tells them
stories, makes a little family.

Part Two

TRAVELERS

TRAVELERS

Is it too late for us to cross the ancient sea
and spend a night beneath the Acropolis?

Now that I've followed you to Dresden
we're more than halfway.

Last week the leaves turned into gold coins
and the river exhaled a veil of mist.

We rode bikes along the Elbe to Schloss
Pillnitz, closed for the winter.

The formal gardens had been plowed under,
but the frescoes, touched again with paint, showed

that someone cared. For once
we were doing something we loved

together. Still, we lost each other riding
the long paths of the gardens.

Through the twilight I spied the red glow
of your borrowed bicycle. We found

each other again at the ferry that carried us
over the dark water toward a rim of light.

When the city heated unbearably in the firebombing,
a woman, eight months pregnant, took refuge in the Elbe

and found it warm as bathwater that February night.
Before we decide where we will be next year,

let us travel to an ancient ruin on a hill, under the stars,
where you've taken me in your stories dozens of times.

Could we live as nomads again, with only the clothes
on our backs, and food for a day?

Or is it too far from the day when you heaved your younger self
out of a riptide—retching but free—onto the sand?

WHAT I SAW IN DRESDEN, JULY 2003

When I tell my friends I'm going to Dresden
they shake their heads and say, "Too bad
we bombed that place." I recall pictures

of rubble. *Slaughterhouse Five.* The Iron Curtain.
But the airport is modern
and the espresso fine. There's a festival

with a ferris wheel and fireworks every night
in the *Altstadt,* where the rebuilt Frauenkirche
dome rises in the process of mending.

Aboard a steamboat, families feast
on coffee, cake, and liqueur in the café.
There's a wedding party on deck

raising their glasses and cheering—I look
in their direction and see a couple making love
on the river bank. Roller bladers glide

along the path at water's edge. Bikers park
under trees, unpack wine and cheese and tablecloths.
An old man wades, buck-naked, into the shallows.

Back in the city, our kids run to join toddlers
dancing in the sidewalk fountains while their
pierced and tattooed parents smoke on the sidelines.

On the tree-lined *Neustadt* plaza at dusk,
skateboarders practice their leaps and turns
on the grand Soviet-style promenade. Parents on bikes

lull their babies to sleep in slings over their hearts.
In a café window we see a miracle—George Bush and
Osama bin Laden, grinning in an act of love.

On our return, I am singled out in the airport
for search and frisk, as though the sensors can detect
the images of freedom I carry home.

THE LANGUAGES OF YOGA IN DRESDEN

On sheepskin mats in our teacher's basement
we breathe the breath of fire, flex
the *hara*, forcefully exhale.

Upstairs the stove hisses and crackles.
Each new sip of air taunts us with the scent of broth
we will not stay to taste. A voice from above

begins to read Russian, lulling us with stories,
sprinkled with soprano accents—our teacher's sons
conversing with *Babushka* from Kiev.

Our teacher, Japanese, speaks German
—*atmen ein—dreissig sekunden mehr*—
so the other students can understand. I chase

the soup's scents—onion, garlic, butter,
tomato, cabbage, beet—until the end of practice
when we chant *Ek onkar. Satnam.*

After the German-speakers take their leave
she invites me to speak English
over steeped green tea.

REPRESENTATIONS OF THE BODY: THE GERMAN HYGIENE MUSEUM
Dresden, May 2010

1.

A bronze giant out front greets all
who approach. We creep
past the daisy-sprinkled lawn,
mount wide stone steps toward
a trinity of giant boxes.

Inside, lofty empty space.
The emptiness is the point.
On one side, the gift shop.
On the other, the Lingner Café,

named for a mouthwash millionaire
who spread the gospel of hygiene.
Delicious cuisine with wine
and beer, if you have the appetite.
Two-story windows allow slabs of light.

2.

Three years after it was built, the Nazis
took over, dismissed its director,
a Jewish woman. She moved to New York.

"We will do away with the old, boring science of statistics,"
Hitler announced. "For the people,

feelings are much more real."
Yes, the museum was implicated
in eugenics, the signs say in German
and English. After the War it was
renamed the Museum of Man.

Much remains untranslated.

3.

The glass woman lifts her arms
and throws back her head as though
opening to the power of knowledge.
Her pedestal rotates and her organs
light up when visitors press buttons
connected by electrodes to labels
for liver, pancreas, heart, lungs,
large and small intestines, uterus.

In the same room a leather vulva
between stumps of legs shows how birth occurs,
a white rag doll dangles by a cord
from slits of folded leather.
Across the aisle, a video plays—
mother panting in a birthing chair,
infant squirming and squalling in the slime
of vernix, blood and shit.

The glass case on the side displays
old slides of embryos, tea stains
in Lucite. At the room's other end:

death masks. In between lie
idealized Greek figurines,
plaster impressions of Aborigines,
models of disease, starvation, obesity.

4.

The next room: the food industry.
In a video the digestive system
pulses; a camera inside the intestines
shows a clean pink passageway washed
constantly with fluid, a water park tunnel.
"*Mann ist was Mann isst.*"

5.

What was your first sex like?
Below the questions, a giant bulletin board-like
display of answers. Paper and pencils are supplied
if you'd like to add an answer. Ads for condoms,
posters for sex education, military precautions:
"I take one of these everywhere I take my penis."
A painting of a crucifix hangs over a blood-stained
sheet, a bucket at the foot of the bed.
A Burka and a chastity belt.

6.

There's nothing left but the brain.
You can put on a headband with electrodes
and compete with another player

to move a silver ball to a goal.
The winner is the one who's most
relaxed after seeing all of this.

FRAUENKIRCHE, DRESDEN

From the rubble, reborn.
Every fallen stone numbered,
then set beside the new. Martin
Luther stands in bronze outside the restored
Cathedral, still named for Our Lady by popular
demand: the woman's church.

From the top balcony I look down
on theology embodied in stone,
an octagonal floor facing a baptismal font
and altar, fronted by a table that holds
an open Bible underneath a simple iron cross.
A priest strolls toward the pews, takes the hand
of a young blond boy, walks him to the table,
shows him how to light the tapers. The organ
with its flourishes, approves. The altar, behind
them, rises in an ornate tableau: Jesus kneeling
in a garden rebuilt from shattered fragments. Above
his head, a cluster of cherubs, golden plums
in buttercream. He cannot see them, though
he begs, "Lord take this cup from me."

Above the altar, across from me,
the organ strains to fill the space. Clerestory
windows of translucent glass remind us of
the transparency of faith. Still further
up, above the instrument, a golden head bowed,
the woman who blesses us all with her lowered gaze:
the agonizing Jesus, priest, boy, congregation, me.

IN GERMAN CLASS

*In memory of Marwa El-Sherbini, d. 1 July 2009 in Dresden,
    Germany*

We learn vocabulary from the news.
Rassissmus our slender teacher writes

on the white board. Still confused
by the German practice of capitalizing nouns, I think

it's someone's name. Like Rasselas.
Agyptische Frau. Egyptian woman.

Auf dem Spielplatz. On the playground.
Our teacher gestures with her arms

to the eight *Auslaender* in her dining room.
War im Gerichtssaal mit einem Messer erstochen.

She was stabbed in the courtroom with a knife.
Schwanger, ermordert vor ihrem Ehemann und Kind.

Pregnant. Murdered in front of her husband and son
by a recently repatriated German Russian who found

her foreign presence offensive when she asked him
to get off the playground swing so her son

could have a turn. He was arrested for calling
her names and couldn't pay the fine.

One of my classmates lifts a tissue to her face.
"You have a cold?" her husband asks.

"No," she says, and goes on weeping.

ENOUGH

"How do you say, 'I've had enough' in English?" my friend Astrid asks. I swirl another bread cube in fondue and laugh. We're both over fifty and shouldn't be anywhere near this much cheese.

"It's a problem in German," she continues. "There's really no way to gracefully refuse food. '*Ich bin Sat*' sounds impolite, like you're stuffed."

"What about just saying '*Ich habe Genug*'?" I've had enough.

"No." She shakes her head. "That sounds like it didn't taste very good."

***

I sit with my sisters on a sunny May afternoon, weeping as we listen to Bach's cantata, *Ich habe Genug*, baritone solo and bassoon mingling with the last of Mother's presence in the emptied apartment.

When her cardiologist said there was nothing he could do for her, Mother stopped eating. Except for the week before she died when I took her to Rachel's Bread for lunch. She ate a whole sandwich: havarti and greens on cranberry wheat berry sourdough.

"That tasted good," she said when she was finished. *Es hat sehr gut geschmeckt.*

THE BUDDENBROOKS HOUSE, LUEBECK

Cross the threshold and enter the text.

Populate these rooms with your own ghosts or
if none appear, open the novel in German or English
and look up the page numbers for both editions
written on cards placed throughout the rooms.

Time condensed into space—Toni's catechism,
the family record book, a sofa where Christian's
unnamed friend once rested. Sheet music for *Tannhauser*
on the organ rack, Hanno's puppet theater set up
on the dining room table. In the "Landscape" room
the red velvet chairs are covered with cloth. Someone's
on their way to remove them. A recording of horse-drawn
carriages plays in the background. The family's long gone.

Over a hundred years and it's not finished—the moment
of transition presented for you, the last and latest guests
of the Buddenbrook family at Mengstrasse 4.
The staircases have been reinforced with concrete
for those passing through.

HERMAN HESSE LEARNS TO PAINT

Montagnola, Switzerland, 1919

*"I have shown my appreciation to the old houses and stone roofs,
the garden wall, the chestnut trees, the near and faraway moun-
tains, by painting, using hundreds of good sheets of drawing paper,
many tubes of water paints, and drawing pencils."*
—Herman Hesse

Outside my window, the sun casts
a thousand shades of green.
Beyond them—stones, hills.
Rooftops sing out burnt sienna,
orange, against a cool wash of blue.
From metal tubes squeeze viridian,
terre verte, chromium oxide, emerald
green onto the palette. Dip the brush
in water, tease a tributary between
gleaming heaps of paint, mix in yellows, blues—
a few dozen shades suggest an infinite range.
War has stolen the language, words
the shards of shattered bridges left behind.
For now, let color play.

NEUROMA

Nerves regenerate,
the hand surgeon tells us,
but if you don't stitch severed nerves
together again they will grow blindly,
seeking reconnection anywhere
they can find it—tangling
with other nerves, growing spirals
around and around themselves
to form excruciating clumps of pain.

The hand is my husband's, his writing
hand, gouged by a broken windshield—
snowstorm, rollover, a one-car accident
that luckily killed no one. The ball-point
sketch is the doctor's, hastily drawn
to illustrate the repair he has made
with a few stitches and invisible thread—
rejoining the tube inside which the nerve
will grow again, a millimeter each month.

It is Sunday morning. We could be
in church. We are in the surgeon's office
and he is taking out the stitches himself,
a rare favor because my husband
is leaving for Frankfurt tomorrow.
The surgeon seems to be enjoying himself,
clean-shaven in his lab coat, smelling of tropical
vacations, waxing like a teacher

to the sound of his own voice, boyish
without his nurses and assistants,
doing what he loves to do.

He gives us a full hour,
breaks open a plaster dressing,
to make a clumsy splint, apologizing
that his lab technician could do it better.
My husband, still dazed with shock, holds
out his bandaged hand, squeezes mine with the other.
My free hand takes notes on aftercare,
a millimeter at a time.

Part Three

SONNETS FOR THE AMISH GIRLS OF NICKEL MINES

.

SONNETS FOR THE AMISH GIRLS OF NICKEL MINES

I.

He tied their legs together, made them face
the blackboard, released their brothers, mothers,
teachers, then barred the doors with two-by-fours.
Ten pairs of toes lined up in place.
Ten pairs of arms could not erase
a moment set in motion by such error.
Ten starched white caps could not conceal their terror
as ten heads bowed in simple grace.
Where once they took their turns to stand apart
and write a sum or sentence they had learned,
(the unprepared might feel some mild concern),
they now could hear each others' beating hearts
as his handgun called the roll—Mary,
Lena, Marian, Anna Mae, Naomi Rose.

II.

Naomi Rose, Mary, Lena, Marian
and Anna Mae—dressed in white by family
and placed in wooden caskets on display
for last loving looks from friends and kin—
now ride in somber carriages again
past the home of him who took their life away
leaving a family puzzled and betrayed
of all they thought he could be as a man.
Their last journey protected by patrol
—even reporters must have a pass—
they move on to church and grave. We are left
without a verse or story to console
us on an autumn day whose shining grass
reflects the sun, a blue sky of clouds bereft.

III.

A blue sky bereft of clouds, wide open
to receive the innocent. But those who live
must have their explanation; the other five
girls recover in intensive care—healed,
they will relive moments of their pain
even as their families seek to reach
beyond the slayer, to his widow, kids.
Though we forgive our debtors, harm persists.
We long for crumbs of consolation
from what survivors remember or will tell
of the unspeakable: the oldest girl
offering to be shot in lieu of others,
her slumped body found beneath chalked letters:
unexpected visitors bring sunshine.

IV.

Unexpected visitors bring sunshine:
the covered casserole still oven-warm,
gleaming jars of produce from the farm
home-preserved: peaches, cucumbers in brine,
blackberry jam, hard-boiled eggs stained with wine
of red-beet juice. This red will do no harm.
This giver's knock brings blessing, not alarm,
an offering to those who've lost in kind.
The scattered toys, the silent house awash
in grief that stunned a family unable
to believe what had been done. The Amish
givers ease the unlocked door ajar and rest
the box of food on the empty kitchen table.
Forgiveness is the unexpected guest.

Part Four

UNEXPECTED GUEST

WHERE TO BEGIN

I can see the pot: blue enameled cast iron,
the one that used to be my mother's,

the weight of the lid sealing in steam, heat, flavors
for decades of family meals. Slow cooking.

When you take the lid off, the poems will come,
my friend Ann tells me. That lid's on tight, I say.

It's glued to the pot with the crystallized juices
of what once bubbled up inside: pot roast

with onions and carrots, coq au vin. Mother's
long gone, and with it her cooking.

What would I see if I lifted that heavy lid now?
A rotting mess like the soup I left in the microwave

for months? The burned carcass of anger?
What home remedies did she use to clean it

without damaging the finish? Baking soda and vinegar?
Bleach? Let it sit under the back porch till the burned

scabs crumble? Here, I haven't even taken off the lid
and already I'm scrubbing it, not even daring

to consider that there could be something
wonderful inside, delectable and ready.

NOT WHAT YOU EXPECTED

When you finally take the lid off the pot,
it's not what you expected.

Not crusted oatmeal burned to the bottom,
not rancid bean soup, or a shriveled carcass.

Lift the lid and inhale sun-warmed fields of lavender,
the moist humus of a terrarium, the tang of perfectly

fermented sauerkraut brine. Something's alive
and growing here—the loaves and fish multiplying

to feed five thousand, bundles of silk scarves
unrolling to clothe a whirling *Draupadi*, never

disrobed. Tiny people crowd through a changing
diorama of miniature cities—one hour Oaxaca

on the Day of the Dead, the next Kyoto, monks
slipping through temple gardens. It's a children's

birthday party on a summer green lawn with games
and prizes for everyone. No tears. Wait, it's an ocean

of tears, with a coastline and rocky cliffs, and you're
diving in with an oxygen tank, sleek amidst the coral.

GUESSING

Among the jars of essential oils in the bathroom, a dainty glass vial of red black liquid. Unlabeled. Its saturated sheen draws me. Rare, royal. *Lydia, the seller of purple.* Where did it come from? Uncork. Sniff. Putrefaction of rotting meat. Heave and gag. Pour the partly liquid, partly coagulated mess down the kitchen sink and rinse, rinse. Stomach rising. Clorox. More hot water. Rinse the vial? No—throw it out. She moved out, left this for me. Her sweet voice answers the phone. I don't ask. It could have been years ago.

STRANGERS

Somewhere above Lincoln, Oregon,
we head up an old logging trail
past manzanita and buckbrush.

Keep Out signs mark gravel driveways
nestled among the ponderosa pines, maybe
marijuana growers we've read about, guarding their crops

with AK-47s. "For every Thoreau, there's an American
with a gun rack," you say. Our foreheads dripping,
lungs woozy from the shallow air, we can say almost

anything. Till we spot fresh paw prints
in reddish clay. Two gigantic German shepherds
bound to our sides, shaking and snorting

into our crotches. I latch onto your arm,
quicken our pace. The dogs, sans collars,
like oversized teenagers, playful and threatening at once.

We quicken our pace, they quicken theirs.
Our talk is reduced to banter, meant to keep
our fear at bay. "At least we're not riding down

the switchbacks in an ambulance."
"At least not yet," you say.
After miles at this pace, we turn

into the driveway of the guest house,
shepherds at our heels. We dash into
the kitchen, bolt the door, panting.

The dogs circle the house for hours.

ON GEOGRAPHY

Once you showed me your secret place,
a long bike ride over hills
past a deserted farmhouse—a hemlock forest

sheltering a flowing stream. Forty years later
and three time zones apart, we pore over
satellite maps on our computers, retracing

our steps amidst cow pies and clover.
Do you see the field shaped like an arrowhead?
Look for the pond just above it to the left.
Your voice in my ears gentle, familiar.

And on the right do you see the winding line through this strip
of woods? I think it's the creek in the hemlock forest.
Last time we hiked together you brought binoculars,

showed me a red-breasted nuthatch, a hermit thrush.
We hiked up the ridge and toured the farmhouse with its
wobbly floors, then to the creek where we and sat in the shade

for hours. I kept your secret till you left. Next week
I will feel the swell of hills without you,
learn whether I am brave enough to trespass alone.

MIDSTREAM

I'm sitting on a boulder in the middle
of a shallow, rushing river

when I catch the gaze of a fisherman
on the opposite bank. We exchange smiles.

He casts his line. It's as though he sees me
in the body of my younger self,

dark hair flowing over slender shoulders,
catching words in my journal with a pen.

The rock's cool hardness presses against me.
Suddenly the gaze is too much. I turn my head

upstream to see what's coming,
downstream to watch the speed of time.

TOPEKA, INDIANA

First shift is over. Semis and horse-drawn buggies
pause at the four-way flashing red light in the center
of town. Amish men on custom reclining bicycles
weave in and out of traffic. One putters along

in a battery-powered wheel chair. Young Amish women
in pastels and head coverings totter into the drugstore
on platform sandals from Walmart. July sun beats
down on all of us. Clouds drift above.

Traffic thins, and the only man in town
who knows who I am hands me the key
to my well-worn Honda, oil fresh and brakes relined,
and I drive home past fields soaked in late-afternoon light.

LESSON, AFTER 9/11

Today the blue sky is empty of clouds
and planes. Sunlight paints triangles

against the insides of my post office box.
No mail. At dusk I walk

with my youngest who points
toward movement at the sky's edge, birds

plumbing the heights with oar-like
wings just beyond the tree-tops.

Stars tremble in violet air.
Not one of the lights in this sky

winks or slowly travels across the horizon.
I tuck my child in bed with *Goodnight Moon,*

then listen to radio reports of vigils
in the streets of New York, strangers

gathering to pray and sing, light candles
that will soon burn out. Yet

a brief light shared in darkness
is all we know. We are forced to learn

at the hands of our enemies.

KNOW WHAT YOU LOVE

The poet tells us,
but it's not easy for some of us.
We know what we should love:
our husbands or wives, our children,
our country, our parents and grandparents,
our friends, our pets.
We must make sure not to love
our spouse's friends too much,
nor our students, nor our
children's friends, either.
The smooth maintenance of society
depends on such restraint.

It's easier to love a blue bowl
filled with light, or the glinting surface
of the Atlantic off the coast of Brittany
with all its chill reflected blues,
something that holds the eyes
but doesn't disturb by loving
—or not loving—back. Something
that yields to the tongue
in bittersweet release,
something like chocolate,
giving pleasure without
so much as an answering
sigh or moan.

UNEXPECTED GUEST

One by one tapers illuminate the faces of singers who gather
in the lofty auditorium to raise their voices to one
deeper and older than their years. Our hearts
swell to admit *a long-expected Jesus*,
when all of a sudden, a bat flies
out of the catwalk
between
the balconies.
It conducts our swaying heads
as it inhabits a space no human can
And the glory of the Lord shall be revealed.
Abruptly the singing stops, doors open. The unwelcome guest
departs. When the doors close and the music resumes, I keep
looking for the bat, longing for the moment
when ll flesh shall see it together.

UNEXPECTED DETOUR

"May I take your hand?" the driver extends a palm
as he inches past us on the outside edge
of a cliff. We are in Donegal, in the Slieve League,

rocks rising 2000 feet over the Atlantic. Nervous strangers
to such rough heights, we laugh, lucky to be on the inside.
When we stop at an overlook to catch our breath, our three-
    year-old

darts up the stony incline like a mountain goat, shrieking
with glee. We follow and follow past dilapidated beehive huts,
runes we cannot read—because he will not stop. We love

his delight at being free. When the rest of us are worn out,
our older son cons him, "This way, this way, up higher,"
chasing him in a downward loop toward the car.

Laughter turns to wailing once he sees the trick.
Back in the car seat, he sobs his heart out.
Fifteen years later, he's become she,

and she's home early from her first year of college,
finishing the semester a paper at a time. I'm leaning
into the cliff in a daily crawl forward.

WHAT YOU TRULY LOVE

Today's sun has left the bedroom too warm for flannels,
so I turn on the air purifier and open windows
for the cross-breeze. It's been a good day.
I've ridden the length of the millrace four times
on my bike. I've sat in the sun, reading. I've dug in the dirt,
made soup, puttered in the kitchen. I've spoken
a few words to Violet, who mostly ignores me for
sleep or her computer. She's supposed to be writing
a paper, but I'm not allowed to make suggestions. Eight
times you've told me to take a bike ride, Mom,
she said. So, I take a ride for both of us to
a spot where I can write. Write about what you truly
love my book suggests, and I write about how much
I love sitting alone in the sun, listening
to the water from the millrace gush through
the pump house pipe and back into the river.
But I have no words for the love
crushed back inside my chest.

EVIDENCE

It's fall break so
I brave the piles
of student papers
I've hoarded.

The students are not
coming back for these
papers. They will never
read my comments.

I remove staples, make
a stack by the shredder,
shove papers through
the narrow feed.

The shredder's teeth devour
my handwriting: *B+,*
has potential but needs
further development.

Like Tibetan monks pouring
the colored sands of their finished
mosaic into a stream, the cycle
continues. Imagine a world

littered with too many sand
paintings, patterns blurred by
careless feet. Imagine my office
filled to the brim with old papers.
The monks don't keep the paintings

because they know the patterns.
My students' learning is still
unfolding. They are no longer

my students. One former student,
a teacher now, calls to tell me,
"The bond between a teacher and
student can never be broken."

I repeat this like a mantra.
The shredder is slow
And the stack is large.

"And guess what? I absolutely love teaching!"

Part Five

LEGACY

LEGACY

"How could you write that?"
she asks me over the phone
after my father's funeral.

She's read the obituary
in which I referred to grandfather's
shunning. How could I not?

It changed our lives.
I could have been an Amish mother
of twelve—or none—depending on whether
I found a fertility doctor worth
his salt. You wouldn't have gone to Teacher's
College. And none of us would have been
saved, I want to add for her benefit. But I don't.

I say, "It's been over sixty years."

When she breaks the silence, it is only
to murmur, "Well, I just don't know why
you had to dig that all up again.
Such shame for the family."

KISHACOQUILAS VALLEY RIDE

When we visit the valley, my Amish cousin hitches up
the mare. Climb in, he says. I take a giant step

into the black buggy—then turn to lift
my sisters up. My cousin lets me sit in front.

We start with a jerk, then swerve onto the road.
Once we've straightened out, he lets me hold

the reins. Feeling grownup and almost Amish,
I'm suddenly shy. It's hard to hear each other

speak—the steel wheels make such a racket
on the road. Looking past the horse's rump

I watch the road crawl under us—fields
part on either side—slow my breath and wonder

how it would feel to live like this, content,
beside my Amish cousin at his pace.

THE GUEST

We didn't want to invite her to the wedding.
We knew she'd come all the way from Kansas
with her beat-up suitcase and stay for weeks,
one family after another hinting that her time was up,
until in desperation they'd buy her a ticket
—bus, train, or plane—
and drive her to the station.

Aunt with the changing last names,
six children given up to foster care: unmet cousins
addresses unknown, even to their mother.
We knew her by her handwriting—a stubborn,
broad-spaced back slant—and the stories we'd been told:
she wet the bed at twelve, never did her chores,
married and divorced the simple-minded hired man.

She came to all the family events—
her camera flashing, oblivious
to taboos—and the family couldn't
refuse to pay her fare. At the anniversary celebration
for our New Order aunt and uncle,
the Old Order guests cringed beneath
raven shawls and dinner-plate hats.

She arrived, short tufts of grey hair framing
a face strong as my father's, and made herself
at home on my parents' couch. For the wedding,
she dug a ruffled yellow dress out of her bags.
Later, when we opened the gifts, we found two dollars
folded into a card scrawled with best wishes
in her unmistakable hand.

THE WOMAN WHO REFUSED TO BE SHUNNED

When the ministers came to the door
in their black Sunday coats
to read her a letter of condemnation,
she ran upstairs and slid under the bed,
watched the light play through the fringe of the spread,
heart pounding until long after the knocking ceased.
After she heard the buggy wheels turn on gravel,
the horses' measured pace, she fell asleep.
She woke as the sun was setting, her face
pressed against the clean wood floor.
She thought she had dozed off in a game
of hide and seek until she remembered.
Like a crepuscular creature
she crept out of her hiding place,
walked softly down the stairs
and out the screen door to the hill
beyond the barn—the place she often went
to dry her hair and watch the sun set.

BARN SKETCH

Outside your painting I'm in the dark
of the barn, looking through the open door
from your point of view. The rough boards
catch the light of late afternoon pouring through.
Beside the stall's dusty window a harness
hangs down in a loop. A rusty can sits on the sill.
The dark that fills the stall is still. No horse
whickers or stomps its hooves. The animals
are gone, so you can sit and linger and look
as long as you like. No chores to do. Just
watercolors and pencils for company.
A visitor now, your car is parked
outside. You can walk through the open
door whenever you choose.

SAFEHOLD

Last night, a double thunderstorm,
July-worthy, in November.

This morning, snow flurries, pixie-dust
of reassurance that the cycles are more

or less in place. But the weather's off—every
month this year another global record-breaker

for heat. And now a charismatic con man's taken
possession of the free world, conspiring with

racists and climate deniers to hasten
the end democracy, of the world as we'd

hoped it. Oh Thou who art many things to
many—how long can we deny the signs?

Like Noah, I build an ark,
gathering what I love inside—

this frail coracle
of words.

FOR THOSE WHO WOULD SAVE THE WORLD

Give up perfection for just one day.
Feel yourself a creature of flesh and bone,
walk around in the cold, wind chafing
your face, joints jarring as your worn
soles pound concrete.
Keep walking till you face
your deepest failure—not
with clenched fists, not blinded
by shame, but with a detached
curiosity that opens to
compassion. Finger
the glazed wound tenderly
as you would caress the gash
in Christ's side. Wear it lightly
as God's fingerprints. You don't
have to travel far to know suffering,
though you may carry it to the end of
the desert before you discover
it's yours. Before you discover the light
failure lets into the darkness.
Polished by forgiveness, our failures
are the only possible windows
through which to truly see.
All else is mirrors
and an endless craving for
a reflection of worthiness.
Remember—Christ was wounded
so he could feel like you.

FABLES

The Father is walking beside a daughter
in a forest with trees of silver
gold and bronze—something like the one

twelve dancing princesses
passed through on their way
to an underground ball.

In the old story, the king spies on his daughters
to learn why they wear out their slippers,
offering death or a bounty of marriage

to the one bold enough to discover the cause.
An old fortune-hunting soldier breaks
branches from each kind of tree

to prove his worthiness. No one hears
the faint cries of the trees except the youngest,
who trembles—the oldest will be his prize.

But in this new forest, on this walk,
Father and daughter move together at a revelatory pace,
absorbing all there is to see. There are no spies,

no tests, no disguise. She carries a camera
to capture reflections of sky in polished leaves.
Looking over her shoulder, he delights in what she sees.

EXCHANGING THE GAZE

"Point both thumbs left," our teacher says, and we
touch palms with those on either side of us—
one hand over, one under—clasp fingers,
find our pace. Across the moving circle,
a man whose body sags with grief, a girl
with glasses and a moonlike face. Our varied
heights and girths and years merge in the pattern
of our steps. I try to feel instead of
watch my feet. Our circle breaks to form a
spiral, crack the whip. "Drop your hands and stop.
Those inside, turn to face a partner
in the outside ring." Pupil of the iris,
I fall into a stranger's eyes—layered
worlds within worlds—then turn the wheel again.

BREATHING LESSON

Raise your arms with the inhale,
exhale and lower them like wings.

Draw energy to your core,
radiate your flame.

Listen to the whirring windmill of the breath
until the charging horse of your heart

nuzzles sweet hay in the barn of your chest.
Become a mountain, then a waterfall.

Bow and kneel, a hero, then, on all fours be
a four-legged: cat, cow, puppy, frog, dolphin, dog;

or a belly-sliding starfish, cobra, sphinx—
open your chest to make more space.

Reach for your feet, become a bow. Turn
and sit to become a staff, twist into Lord

of the Fishes—half; slide forward
as a pigeon, or squat and balance as a crow.

Rise as warrior, goddess, dancer, tree.
If you like, turn upside down. Release

into child. Roll over a happy baby,
fingers grabbing onto feet. Extend

onto your back, imitate the dead.
Let gravity absorb your weight.

DANCING WITH MENNONITES

A guest at this feast of cider
and laughter, I watch my toddler
scramble up steps of baled hay

as my older children leap to join circles
at the call of a fiddle and two guitars,
fling themselves into

the swings and steps
of a Virginia reel as a crazy
preacher calls out the steps,

models kick-turns. Teens in jeans
lock arms and spin parents and grandparents,
exchange and release inside and outside

until the caller calls out to me.
My toddler surrounded by friends,
I join the last dance, raise my hands

to one whose palms lift me
above my heavy, stumbling clogs,
airy skirt of Indian gauze

and find myself at home.

ACKNOWLEDGMENTS

I am grateful to the editors of the following publications for printing some of these poems, often in earlier versions or under different titles: *Adanna, Atlanta Review, Bluestem, The Cresset, Limestone, The MacGuffin, The Mennonite, Monarch Review, Nimrod International Journal, Quiddity, Perspectives, Poet Lore, Porcupine, Rhubarb Magazine, The Stickman Review, Valparaiso Poetry Review, Vision, Washington Square Review.* Gratitude also to the editors of anthologies that published some of these poems: *Making Poems: Forty Poems with Commentary by the Poets, The Poetry of US, Tongue Screws and Testimonies,*

Thanks to Jeff Gundy, editor of Cascadia's DreamSeeker Poetry Series, who worked with me on the final polishing of this manuscript; to Michael A. King and Cascadia Publishing House for giving a home to this book in the Dreamseeker poetry series; to Goshen College for Mininger Center Grants that enabled the development of this work.

Earlier versions profited from generous readings by Todd Davis, Elizabeth Falcon, Laura Hostetler, Joan Houlihan, Mary Hoyt, Julia Spicher Kasdorf, Ada Limon, Adrian Matejka, Martha Rhodes, and Shari Miller Wagner. B. H. Fairchild, Carolyn Forche, Helen Frost, Rebecca Gayle Howell, Ilya Kaminsky, and Emilia Phillips offered comments on individual poems. My online Wompo Workshop group has witnessed and assisted at the birth of many of the poems: Wendy Carlisle, Patricia Fargnoli, Ann Fisher-Wirth, Louisa Howerow, Athena Kildegard, Alicia Ostriker, Penelope Scambly Schott, Barbara Taylor, and more.

My students have offered challenge and delight. To my sisters, my children, their partners, and my grandchildren, thanks for the support and love. To my husband, gratitude for living the journey with me, for encouragement and support, and so much more than words can say.

THE AUTHOR

Ann Hostetler, Professor of English, Goshen (Ind.) College, is the author of *Empty Room with Light* and editor of *A Cappella: Mennonite Voices in Poetry*. She edits *The Journal for Mennonite Writing* at www.mennonitewriting.org.

CPSIA information can be obtained
at www.ICGtesting.com
Printed in the USA
FFHW021656180319
51124999-56572FF